PAPER SCISSORS STONE

PAPER SCISSORS STONE

KIT FAN

香港大學出版社
HONG KONG UNIVERSITY PRESS

Hong Kong University Press
14/F Hing Wai Centre
7 Tin Wan Praya Road
Aberdeen
Hong Kong
www.hkupress.org

ISBN 978-988-8083-47-3

British Library Cataloguing-in-Publication Data
A catalogue record for this book is available
from the British Library.

10 9 8 7 6 5 4 3 2 1

Cover © Ffiona Lewis, 'Curlew in Flight II'

Printed and bound by Kadett Printing Co. Ltd.,
Hong Kong, China

for
Hugh Haughton

*A is building with building-stones: there are blocks,
pillars, slabs and beams. B has to pass the stones,
and that in the order in which A needs them. For this
purpose they use a language consisting of the words
"block", "pillar", "slab", "beam". A calls them out; – B
brings the stone which he has learnt to bring at such-
and-such a call. – Conceive this as a complete primitive
language.*

Wittgenstein

Scissors should always be sold, they should never be given.

A Dictionary of Superstition

*Paper, as opposed to Egyptian papyrus, was first made
by the Chinese eunuch Cai Lun from the bark of trees,
remnants of hemp, rags of cloth, and fishing nets.*

The Four Great Inventions of Ancient China

CONTENTS

How Cangjie Invented Chinese Characters

'*The moment Cangjie invented the written words, the sky rained millets as nature's secret was disclosed, and the ghosts cried through the night as their shapes could no longer be changed.*'

– The Book of Huai-nan Tzu (2 BC)

In the beginning was the knot,
and the knot was on the branch,
and the knot was mine, the same
tree on the same bank of the same
river, and I tied a second one,
and none of them had names.

Then all things began twice:
the river, the bank, the tree, the branch.
At first sight, I was still on my own.
My shadow followed me home.

By the tree laden with knots,
I washed my face and a phoenix
flew across the ripples round my knees.
I turned and found a creature
that had fallen from its beak.

I made a knot and sat by the river
till my shadow lengthened behind me.

As I looked at the hoof-print,
a passing hunter said, 'It's a *Pi Xiu*,
the ninth offspring of a dragon!'
He walked past, following his shadow.
I walked home, following mine.

But there were currents in the river,
trails on the banks; there was the crown
of the tree, the fork of the branch.

The same was in the beginning
with the mouths of the knots,
their braided muscles kept tight
through last night's storm.

This morning I loosed them
one by one into the river, each ripple
a quiver of unnoticed past
scratched on a tortoise shell,

from the first knot of spring
to that of yesterday's phoenix.

Pictures of Foreign Objects

A candle stands in its holder
while the matches sleep in their box
both evenly pressed on paper
opening to a book like a butterfly
sunning its wings
in a glass box on a pedestal
at the corner of a building
once known as the British Library
you happened to visit in some past
life to look at the letters
of a dead poet whose letter *t*
stands oddly on its hooked feet
while the *s* sleeps snug
at your desk through the storm
of the hours tick-tocking
back in time to the second story
of the British Library
where you might still be there
deciphering the letters
and the dates
while I might still be standing
at the site of St. Pancras
or the green of Russell
Square and we might
still be walking to the LRB
though the British Museum

might no longer
be there
and the Thames might still
take us to the unlit bridge
to Elysium?

The Hairdresser by the Styx

Don't ask for a second chance: it is a relief
to live the same life again. What is beautiful
in repetition is not the false belief
in suffering, nor something as simple
as pure coincidence. All the things
that I saw, heard, breathed, touched, and ate.
For instance, an instant. All the beings
that I met I meet again. Some are late,
others early. In a story like this, I can't bear
to imagine the difference between the past
and the future. It is not present here.
Everything is the same and all is not lost.
Trust me, I spent most of my life in the mirror.
I do partings well. Loosen the tie. Undo the collar.

Roots

'... slowly we ran out of rations, started digging
in abandoned gardens for potatoes, taros, half
trampled carrots. At gunpoint they shuffled us
out of the shop, took the metalwork and money;
the shelves, the drawers, all emptied in a blink
of an eye too scared to look. It could have been
January or March, three or four days, roaming
inland, gathering what was left in the soil.
Grassroots, earthworms went into the broth,
thickened with a handful of rice and salt.
We tried mud to stop the rumbling. It worked
with loose stools. Three years and eight months
before the sun on the white flags finally set.
Luckily your mother was born four years later ...'

Thatched House Destroyed by an Autumn Storm

after Tu Fu

In September, on a high-sky autumn day,
the gale's howl blows the heavy thatch
from the house. Straws fly across
the bank, scatter in the fields;
some hang in the upper branches, some swirl
and sink in the puddle-ponds.
Knowing I am old and frail, the children
from the southern village gang together
openly, gathering the reeds in their arms,
and disappear into the bamboo forest.
I shout and scream, but they don't return.
I walk home, leaning on my walking stick,
talking to myself.

The wind drops.
The ink-clouds turn the autumn sky
into a dark desert. The threadbare quilt
is cold as iron. My son's not sleeping well;
he kicks and tears the quilt.
The bed's wet, the house leaks, there's nowhere dry.
The rain's tight as linen, won't stop.

It's been hard to sleep since the war began,
these long wet nights, and no sign of dawn.
I wonder how many houses we'd need to build

to shelter the world's poor.
A mountain weathers every storm.
Will such houses ever see the light of day?
If I could see them, I think I'd die happy,
here in the cold, under this thatch.

In a Pavilion by a Stream

after Tu Fu

In a pavilion by a stream
I loosen my sleeves and bare my belly,
looking over the field and reciting poems
from memory. The heart has no wish
to keep pace with the stream.
Clouds move slowly through the mind.

There's not much to see in late spring:
everything that went has come back.
I think of the home I can't return to.
Bored, I go back to poetry.

Hero Tree

From the classroom window,
the summer's aorta revives in the dark
hero tree. Bark ideogram,
ember-tinted, no trace of leaves.
A family of four cicadas homes in
on its tall ebony nakedness:
something for a long summer song.

The white chalk stub U-turns
on the wide blackboard, hissing out
a map of Confucian morphemes:
stone-classics that were chiselled
for *the eye looking straight into the heart.*

Fans spin overhead, ripe dozy hours.
Our heads bow, fishing for cancelled
valleys lost to the Yangtze River Dam.

China Landscape in the Forecourt of the British Museum

It's easy to invent a land and easier to efface it.
But not now, not right here as five Catalan boys
are hiding their faces in the leaves of the handkerchief tree
teasing the name of this ancient, once endangered species
on the sixth of July this year at a quarter past three.

I love the sound of their language, the idleness it carries
in the summer haze. The steps, the pillars, the beauty
of stationary things, and the heart-shaped handkerchief
fluttering effortlessly like the ghost of a dove.

Three minutes late. The bamboo hisses like a boiling
kettle; the white mulberry misses the silkworms;
the lily listens to the weeping willow.

Not having seen each other for nearly two years
one assumes civility if not closeness.

I sit by the scholar's rock, deciphering the word

Though set in stone, the dividing strokes hesitate
at the meeting points, at the ink crossroads

where meanings travel – blossoms, China –
somewhere unrecognisable as the gentle terraces
of paddy fields, on the first of many journeys

to 'the motherland'; so much water so close to home
but we chose to go away, so that we could be together
as a whole, the four of us, a busy family fuelled
by an itinerary through many sites and cities.

The night before I left home, sleep visited you both
with a gift of snores, as my room filled up with walruses.
Then I hear one of the boys scream *'Mummies!'*
in English and you appear at the gate, weaving through
the boisterous crowd, waving to me with your handkerchief.

Paper Scissors Stone

I

It is not only the guilty secrets
are hard to tell in the end.

From the age of six my mother
put me in the Telford Gardens

Library in Kowloon so that she
could sweat in other people's

kitchens. That was why I owned
a library corner. Every shelf

hour held me in custody.
Page travels, lost milk teeth

and pre-myopia. Curled up
in my shell in the sun with Little

Red Riding Hood and King Midas,
month by month I crawled

like a snail past spines of fairy
tales, before I knew the Moon

Goddess, the dragon dance,
dandelion and chrysanthemum.

There were years of afternoons,
clouds and thunders, without

parents. I dreamed of an orphan-
age: long corridors, dorm beds, wet

sheets, breathing up against the wall.
I made myself homeless as if she

would never come back, her hands
tinted with bleach.

I prayed that my book-lined
womb would not be scissored apart

as pages and covers braced the skin
against the emperor's new clothes.

II

And I wasn't totally wrong.
That August seven years ago

the library was torn down
like many other things.

No trace now of books or shelves
or readers. Only dust, pits,

cranes and stones. The limbs
of Orpheus are not there.

Even though guilty secrets
are hard to tell, I wish you

could have told me why paper
attracts scissors, books turn to stone.

BN(O)

I

It was 1987 when my grandmother and I
lined up in the stomach of a long queue

right in front of the British Consulate
at the junction of Supreme Court Road

and Justice Drive on the pre-handover
Hong Kong Island. It was another

subtropical summer day. The air tasted
of storms and breathlessness. Long hours

of cicadas' buzz lengthened the equatorial
idleness. Holding a dark umbrella against

the hammering sun, my grandmother
struggled to peel an orange – she thought

with confidence – that would ease
the heat of my sweaty body.

She sub-divided it into little segments
and gave them to me one by one as the line

crept towards the front teeth of a building
as big as the Battleship Potemkin. The sour

tear-like orange was there like a clove
of garlic melting in my mouth. It wasn't

a time for complaints and nobody
murmured a word of discomfort. It was

the silence of refugees longing for an identity
foreign to this tiny, floating, motherless city.

II

Years after my grandmother died of old age
and solitude, I'm now waiting again at the head

of a long queue in front of the immigration
desks at Heathrow Airport. There is no sun,

no umbrella, no cicada. Just me and my passport.
To the impassive official, I hold out this bruised

dark red travelling document, product of 'One
Country, Two Systems'. I am again abandoned

by two countries, between two continents.
I walk towards the desk with rehearsed apathy.

There is a familiar taste of orange sourness
running on the tongue, swallowed by the stomach.

From a Distance

The narrator who comes from nowhere
sits among us disguised as someone
you wouldn't think would lie. He opens
his mouth like a book, picks a story
from the so-called 'mementos of memory'.
For ease of future reference, he calls

it 'From a Distance' like the bird calls
at daybreak. But the story is nowhere
closer than the horizon, and his memory
never slips: 'It's near midnight. Someone
and his mother are listening to a story
on the radio next door. She opens

the cupboard full of bags, which opens
on more bags. With telephone disconnected, no calls
will disturb her husband's early shift.' 'The story,'
he says, 'is about a home factory nowhere
in particular but specific to that someone
who is unwilling to forgo the strange memory

of his mother's night shift at home, the memory
of her putting thread through a hole that opens
on a price tag to be attached to clothes. "Someone
might not notice but that's work." The way she calls
it *work* implies that there is nowhere
like this home, nothing more real than the story

of a mother sitting on a wooden stool, telling a story
at midnight to her son about work.' 'In his memory,'
he says, 'there is The Buddha of Laughter from Nowhere
holding his belly up on the shelf, who opens
his big mouth but doesn't break the silence. He recalls
a shadow moving on the street. There's someone

walking home along the lampposts, someone
like him, a stranger to any home or story
who happens to be feeding thread as the first bird calls
the last dawn back, sewing up each hole in memory
of the stories on the radio next door. Each opens
onto a drawer full of bags and price tags.' 'Nowhere,'

the narrative opens, 'is where each story
goes.' After the curtain calls, he imagines someone
lost to memory, still looking nowhere.

Reading Thom Gunn's Notebooks at the Bancroft Library

for H.H.

Let's talk about Gunn.
Not *Thom*, not the one haunted by Charlotte
Thomson Gunn since she gassed
    herself when he was fifteen.
            (See 'The Gas-poker' in *Boss Cupid*.)

But *Gunn*, the anonymous.
'The dead poet.' 'The Prince of Cats.' Not nine
lives but one. *'Who am I speaking to /*
    in this poem / if you are not here?'
            'Here' being this seat at the edge

of this table, from the window
all this green sharpens under the sun – redwood,
eucalyptus. It is finally California.
    'How hard is it for me / to believe
            being in this place / when I am already here?'

('Along the Simplon's steep
and rugged road'.) The campanile strikes – *one* –
from a distance it looks like the one
    in Piazza San Marco in Venice –
            (sshh) listen, it strikes again – *one*.

Twice, hourly, turning
the pages back. The first cyclotron and
plutonium; californium and berkelium;
        the first sketches for the atomic
                bomb *here* among these emerging groves.

        Read on.
It's a question of Gunn and his notebooks
as manuscripts mean handwriting
        mean a presence of someone
                long gone but now '*here*' again

        hissing on these pages.
'Hissing', not yet speaking, like the tail of a cobra
cautious long enough, about to strike.
        It's nearing five. The clouds
                have just come in near the campanile.

        They too, are about
to strike. *One, one.* A click, a raindrop.
This divided country where the two sides
        of its continent cannot look up
                but hear the growing emptiness within.

        '*Tell me if you can /*
what is within you?' 'You' being neither a *Thom*
nor a *Gunn*; being the *you* you know best,
        the *you* like most *yous* are, whatever
                they mean in different circumstances.

What is *within* you
that makes you lie on the floor at home alone,
and think of pills, high buildings, a
river, car crash or heart attack?
What makes you time the untimely act?

It must be nearing five.
*'Why do I always think ahead / of time even though / it
has no head or tail?'* The library's closing
early for 'seismic renovation'. *The moving
ground; / these manuscripts / above soft vibrations?'*

'Here it is a mix
of sunshine and hail, wild light bursts and knife-
like gusts of wind', you wrote in an email,
'I have planted salad, rocket, parsley,
spinach and even a couple of tomato plants.

But otherwise
have been reading, writing, playing Beethoven
and Shostakovitch on the piano.' I walk out
of the library, pass the campanile.
It's good to think of your hands digging

in the soil and piano.
'Isn't it supposed to be about / Gunn and his notebooks?'
On the platform to the Bay Area, there's
a man who opens his palms to the sky,
follows me into the coach and sits opposite.

He sings, he murmurs.
'Why is it hailing in May?' He's talking to me.
He opens his palms; he glares at me,
   humming something resembling
      human speech: 'I know you don't smile,

you don't speak.
But that's the way I get to know you. You know
I'm all on my own.' *'Is it democracy / when*
   there is no one / to vote for?' I've to look
      away. *'What makes you stop writing / but go on drinking*

and picking up / homeless junkie
boys for your bed?' You don't stop. *'Will there be a last salmon?'*
You open your palms. *'Wasn't that an earthquake or a bomb?'*
   'Hasn't the bell struck?' Again to the sky. *'What*
      is left to read?' *'Tell me why / why the bell is still / still?'*

Handwriting

for T.K.W.

To start with O'Connell Bridge and the River Liffey *(leaning
over on my stomach on August stone looking down)* the currents
drawn by sunlight *(this choking weight, feet in mid-air)*
like the day in Jack Yeats's 'The Liffey Swim', whose coral
colours' nervy flow you've never seen *(dropping, ending it)*.
To continue with All Hallows Church now called
St. Andrews *(the cold smell of sacred stone called him)*:
'No Communion Today'. Then walk southward along
Westland Row retracing those footsteps to Sweeney's
following the guidebook *(sending you the sweet lemon soap?)*.

After a rest, it is time for the Book of Kells *(my books
were never your kind of books)* and a closer look at its illuminated
vellum leaves: one bears a Buddha-like Madonna
with the child cupped in her arms *(his teal-blue top just like
the fish-jade you carry round your neck for peace)*. A page-palette
of colours: iris, lilac, egg yolk and lapis lazuli
brushing against the lagoon of a Latinate 'g'.

Curtains drawn, a desk with a chair: it is time to start.
~~*(This postcard is a page from Book of Kells?)*~~ In the end
you'd written: 'Though we won't see each other again,
this is meant to last.' *(It did last, hidden in my wardrobe among
your presents.)* I should have gone on (all the way from you to here).

This is Dublin *(how clearly your handwriting comes to mind before I can remember your face).* Outside, the human traffic dapples the busy street *(this silence between us).* Inside, two angels flutter in the background behind her halo *(those shell-like feathers started clopping)* and I stop.

Watershed

In time my story will hinge on this host
of conifers hissing on the banks every single
movement of the night you can scarcely tell
what century it is the river the pale sad faces
from the past at an awkward angle the new moon
staring out at the ribbon of road spilling downhill
into a labyrinth as if to say you take
all the decisive steps in your life as a result
of slight inner adjustments of which you're barely
conscious the loud the soft that pitch of call
among foliage swallowed up by a wavering shadow
how to put one foot in front of the other
what if it was just a twig in the field the fog
the hours on the walls streaming down the fort
the grey rigid uniform the props the ghost
in me waiting for the candles to be lit:
Who's there? Stand and unfold yourself.

Obstacles to Dreams

'We are such stuff as dreams are made on'

— The Tempest

Under the dogwood
in the brambles
two cardinals singing
in the calm before the storm

Too early for butterflies
but not for the snails
waiting by the ferns

Drunk you lie low and snug
murmur a few words
and turn on your other side

Between the acts of sleep
and rage you will raise
your voice for the part –

we shall lose our time
and all be turned to barnacles –

You will age and love the sea

Grasping the nettle by a stream
I am made of air not skin

Lines from 'Another Poem of Insomnia'

Once the curtain's been drawn, the restless bed swings
    between the room and the hours, like a boat cutting through
        a storm. The world is suddenly darker like a cave within a
        cave.

'Why do I say "like", pretending that it's something else?'
    It's the sixth time in half an hour you turn and look for
        a better place. As if here were the shore of a life that you
        do not own.

But you're not asleep. However well you pretend
    as in the day for money and family, or at work. *'I am*
        sorry it's only a quasi-lullaby; insufficient to guard the bones
        cast up on the shore.'

Now you turn to my side, slipping your hand here onto my plain
    bony chest, relaxed into our nakedness and wakefulness. *'I put*
        my hand on top of yours.' The shriek of a motorbike's muffled
        behind the curtain.

Suddenly we're here again, unafraid of storms or caves.
    The world smells of dark, thick, flammable tar. Listen.
        Pit-pat. This isn't my heart. *Pit-a-pat.* How can it be
        a harbour?

A Letter to Woyzeck

I wake and search that phrase
   in every thought I have. I sit in the chair where you always sit,
and mediate between the window and
   the mirror. Or practise saying *I* until I can breathe without it.

The sun writes left to right,
   crossing the furniture accumulated into the likeliness of home:
the dripping tap, the torn-rimmed jug,
   floor brush, and handmade wooden crib.

It is the objects we own that make
   life barren. I know if I look through the window, there is a world
made of heaps of bone but if I look
   into the mirror there's a window, a world of glass where nothing

can be seen through.
   There are times in the afternoon I move the mirror towards the crib,
beaming the sun's reflection
   onto his sweaty face, listening to those tears fall into place.

There are streetlamps and batflights.
   There are puddles and tunnels, clocks and coffins. There are
times and places we once
   dwelt in but don't belong to anymore. But what is there *there*

for you, Woyzeck? The sky's
   wheel? The cloud's orbit? And what's it like, this living once

reduced to a few words that haunt
tracts of a lifetime still too strange for the tongue to touch?

Steady, Woyzeck. There's no word
without a rhyme. There's the murmuring in the mud. There's
the silence that disintegrates you into parts,
bits and scraps, the fly sitting on the back of your palm.

There's the sound of the ebbing river,
pebbles taking refuge after the glacier's final shove. There's
me lowering myself in next to you,
hands loosened, a shell the storm has cast up on the strand.

Ghost Letter

Dear Father –

To speak is to blunder but I venture
since the pen is for saving things
from chaos. This moment I call
the present, in the midst of a storm,
in the winter of my years, I open
my mouth, breathe lightning
to reply to you, as the ink is open
to the pen, the pen to the hand,
the hand to the heart. The door
you shut, the truth stuck
in my throat, a sentence you left
unfinished. Without elegance,
metre and rhyme, I write, as closely
as I can, from this dark room
to the moment I call the past.
The rain has finally come.

Images, not words, float around me.
They are eyes staring at me
into which I am forced to stare back.

If you once saw a bullet
hit a bird, I was the stranger
who built the heart.

Where's home?
A stunted apple tree, a mossy stone?

I have lived, like you, a life
of barely believable vacuity.
I still want to paint. My best paintbrushes
were all eaten up by moths.

Mother died three months after you.

It's only now I am convinced
that the problem of the *Phaedo*
is whether the soul is of the same nature
as things that are born and die.
It fills me with pity that you of all people
should be unable to read such a beautiful thing.

But Heaven, I hear, is a sequestered place.
This austere afternoon will end
before the last drop of tallow
swallows the candlewick.

Yesterday, a mason mended
your garden walls with new bricks.
The world is only a half-
way house; though unbeheld,
it's foliage softly adds –

Your belated daughter
Katharina Pompilia
This 21 May, A.D. 1669

Rain on a Spring Night

after Tu Fu

It seems the kind of good rain
that knows the season. It happens
in spring when everything happens.
It follows the wind that slipped in with
night. It moistens everything soundlessly.

Ink-clouds drain down the village
road. Lights burn in the empty boats.
In the morning drenched red branches
will arch over the city of Chengdu.

The Gardener of Qufu

The pine bark had cracked open
earlier in the autumn frost and now a late train
of ants heavy with tyre dust crossed a word I once carved
on the trunk hauling bits of rice crackers
up along the frozen aqueduct
to the treetops where you caught your sleeve
in the needles, fell

and broke you back sixty-seven
year ago while I was playing with my first marbles
in the clearing outside the temple and I turned around the miniature
yew and kumquat, mountains and pavilions
all thrown out of place, places
I dreamt were real because the garden
was a prison.

You spent the next month restoring
the landscapes in the pots while I jumped over
the iron gate, swishing past the giant stone tablets incised with
the Master's words, inching under the dark
foliage before the path opened
my eyes to the mountain where I practised
writing on the trunks

with my penknife and disappeared
when the fog rose. Then I'd wade homewards,
drunk with the secrets of the day, and see your thinning hair

messed up during your siesta before you asked
me if I had tossed the manure
and washed the tablets, ten thousand things
simplified into the one routine.

Now only the routine's left:
being both here and not here speaking
as if one could really speak of roots at our meeting place.
Now we are quiet at last I can forgive you.
Remember 'the sky' I once
scratched on that tree? Perhaps you
can forgive me?

Morandi

Wrestle with the object first.
Then plant the shadow.

The Enigma of a Cul-de-sac

after Giorgio de Chirico's *Ariadne*

I once guided those steps with thread
and now the shadows come.

They enter the arcades and rest
diagonally under the grey facades.
I look at the shade behind the pillar
under the arch, as I did before,
as if time were material.

At this time of day the piazza is empty again.
Two men walked past five seconds ago.
They're still walking past.
When time is material
everything matters.

I was abandoned once but now I recline
here on the sun-drenched pedestal,
one hand on my temple.
I've slept lives away in the shade.

If I doze for long enough, will the thread
that unravelled his maze, unravel mine
in its ponderous marble sack?

'Last night wind rose'

after Li Shang-Yin

Last night's wind rose
    under last night's constellations.
My Lakeside Gallery looks west
    while your Cinnamon Hall faces east.
I don't have phoenix wings
    to fly over to your side
but a touch of the magic
    rhino-horn will re-unite us.

Sitting beside me you passed me
    a jade glass full of spring wine,
and we tried to guess
    the riddles flickering on the red lanterns.
On sentry duty at dawn I listen out
    for the drum-call to attend the court.
Setting out on horseback for the minister's,
    I drift like a hollow straw.

Hammershøi

At first the room was still dark till a ray
of sun landed on my feet, lightened after sleep.
Empty-headed, I took my time in bed, listening
to your downward flight, each naked step
eliciting a syllable from the stairs of what the house
wouldn't tell. How we found each other here,
leaving our small islands for this bigger one
to learn, work, love, and root. It was late morning
or already noon. A bus went past. The dust
motes were dancing in the sunbeams the way
they do. One and two and three – each speck
drawing the light – a room painted white,
a handleless door, the sun framed in the twenty-
four glass panes on Hammershøi's windows.

Eros at the Gym

'I invited him to the gymnasium with me, and exercised with him there, thinking I might make some progress that way. So he exercised and wrestled with me, often completely on our own, and (needless to say) it got me nowhere at all.'

— Plato, *The Symposium*

My timing is simple:
your eyes are wide open
as the eucalyptus glistens
in the sun and your eyes
are closed as you listen
to each leaf in its glassy case
keeping in mind the idea
of sunset as an ordinary
thing like moonrise or thirst
after the taste of anchovy
and when your eyes
are open again it is Socrates
three feet away about to strike
but four months later you will
describe in your own words
someone bitten by an adder
in the worst possible place
in a heart or soul
somewhere dark and moist
one summer evening
shelling broad beans
from their beds

Four Treasures of the Scholar's Studio

*'The Emperor Ai of Han was sleeping in the daytime with
Dong Xian stretched out across his sleeve. When the
emperor wanted to get up, Dong Xian was still asleep.
Because he did not want to disturb him, the emperor cut
off his own sleeve and got up.'*

–'Passions of the Cut Sleeve',
Records of the Grand Historian

I

In the nick of time you hand over the bow
tear off your sleeve hold me in a blindfold
Close your eyes my dear as if you were looking
at the past through a glass mountain
Your fingertips spine-head and the shaft
of the arrow between our hands a stir
in the shrub Now you whisper and I release
my breath the two of us here disembodied
reduced to the enlarged pupils of our eyes
the smell of the mist rises the path downhill
swerves my thought says you will be gone
in two days and I will soften the hare's purple
hair in its blood wind-dry it overnight
and bind it with silk paint with lacquer
marry with a handle of the best bamboo
in the land so next time you write the brush
will be keen as a knife and in time I will decipher
the true meaning of your characters

II

Not far out of earshot the season of felling
pines in the hillside arrived in the courtyard
each strike a throb my heart lingered behind
the screen and you came closer undressed all false
pretences gone in an instant the pines
turned into soot mixed with gold cinnabar
the ink stick hidden in my sleeve the brush
I took to wash in the pond where I practised
your words move of your wrist each stroke
on water stained my mind pondered
another eye shone through a mirror
Now three months later in pure coincidence
you turn to me and ask why the lotus
has grown so dark I am a pool of frozen water
a black froglet dives into the shade

III

On the third night our eyes met on the spur
of the moment deep frost clutched the roof
tiles room within room lanterns flickering
Lock the door behind you said and slipped
the ink stone into the collar against my chest
sparks went down my spine and your sleeve
held across my lips whispering Stay there
the smell of candles far from home
the warm stone in your palm the ink stick
in my hand our tears sour as snowdrops
All these you said form the base of good ink
All I saw was the muddy shale a brush
of thick clouds was all I thought I saw

IV

In a split second your handwriting sinks
out of sight my sleeve lingers at your desk
the brush sits inkless on the stone I sit
in the chair you always sit in reading your letter
word by word a boat on a soft tide
will return in two days the snow will fall
and what came across that spring
in the most literal sense of the word
Now this winter a fire a foot away opens
the ground and takes hold of the dry leaves
while in your own hand each character
burns through the paper sinks out of sight
second by second in that first split second

Night Temples

Four is the hour you often turn to books.
First you lie flat, both hands on the bed,
then in slow motion, your shoulders, chest,
stomach, navel, and, finally, waist
slip out of the dark duvet, a luna moth
emerging from a silk cocoon. Then
the clicks of bones, lamp, clock.

I've to sleep through storms but still half notice
your rituals of wakefulness. It could be
the slightest movement; a page turned,
margins scribbled on, the occasional hum.
It could be none of these but my own internal
rhythm, knowing to wake, when you're awake.

Once (months or years ago) I thought
I was asleep but heard and remembered
your need for 'a convincing temple'
where you could kneel, pray, or cry.

I didn't reply but turned back to my side,
thinking of all the temples in all the places
we had visited. The one in Tai O on Lantau Island
its walls so damp one could barely read
the names of their ancestral fishermen.
A tiny clay shrine housed the Goddess of Mercy.
It was dawn. A cormorant caught an eel.

Our homage to Bunting took us to Sedbergh.
I left you in Briggflatts Meeting House,
all on your own, listening in the silence
to the state of its maker's mind.
When I returned you weren't there.
It was early morning. A ray of sun
shone through the plain glass – the dancing
dust, the remoteness of death –
a place worshipped by a boy and again
when he grew old. You were outside
by a row of Quaker tombstones,
and left a sea shell there on one of them.

It was only on feast days the patients
in St. Janhospitaal in Bruges could see
Memling's angels playing a lute and lyre
on the saddle roof of St. Ursula's Shrine.
In the midst of the massacre, they too
would have noticed a couple: a man,
troubled, holding a fur hat to his chest,
while a woman, frowning deeply, prayed
with clutched hands. Not a single cloud
in the broad daylight. It was too early or too late.

It must be six when you turn off the light,
rock the boat and bury your head in my chest.
I stroke your face and kiss your temple
until your breath sails calmly on towards
the horizon as the sun rises in Ithaca.

'Chinese Poetry' (in translation)

'Last night's wind rose / under last night's constellations.'
And you weren't there. You came from a small village where mountain

after mountain after mountain held the spring fog.
You returned for a visit by bus. To study 'holding

forth' (what Confucius called 'gentleness'). 'Warm and soft / heavy
and broad: / the teaching of poetry.' *You yourself couldn't say why*

you were here again. The family sitting opposite you
in the bus was reading a brochure about the place

you were born. 'Withered wisteria, aging tree and dusk crow /
Small bridge; water flows by people's homes / Old road, west

wind, thinning horse / The sun's in the west /
We, torn apart, are scattered near the land's end.'

You were once well travelled. From the North to the South, you'd climbed
all the 'famous' mountains. Now you were lost in your own.

The road smelt of wet wood and mushroom.
Your trainers went splish-splosh in the mud.

'A pinch of rice / a sip of water / lie down / my arm / for a pillow /
Like this / Like joy / in loneliness … / Like me / this moving cloud.'

You paused on the missing beat.
You tripped on an unstable stone.

You hurt your knee but not too badly. You sat down. *The strokes*
came together
into characters: 'water / flow / heart / no / chase / clouds / here /

mind / slow'. It is Tu Fu, you thought,
in English. As good as it could be.

'Could be': the way this language fostered possibility in the past tense.
The way you were spelling everything out and keeping your lips

tight, your mother tongue. Sitting here,
you found the stream and the clouds.

'The heart has no wish / to keep pace with the stream.
Clouds move slowly in your mind.' *And 'in your mind'*

you thought they were slow, yet could they be
moving even slower than you thought?

Nothing seems to resolve, but then 'nothing' is a resolution.
You sat here. And so it was. *Letting the stream run and the clouds*
move.

「山窮水盡疑無路　柳暗花明又一村」
You walk on. The traveller's left behind.

NOTES

'Pictures of Foreign Objects' is the title of an exhibit
in *From East to West: Traditional East Asian and
Contemporary European Printing* at the British Library in
2008. LRB is the London Review of Books Bookshop on
Bury Place near the British Museum.

'Thatched House Destroyed by an Autumn Storm', 'In a
Pavilion by a Stream', and 'Rain on a Spring Night': Tu
Fu wrote these poems in AD 761, when he was 50. He
had escaped capture and been forced into exile after
the Tang dynasty had been torn apart by An Lushan's
rebellion (AD 755–759). He drifted from town to town,
witnessing bombed farmhouses, unfed children and
mutilated corpses. Sick and utterly impoverished, he
arrived at Chengdu, Sichuan in October 759. He spent
several weeks without any shelter, before earning enough
money to set about building a simple thatched house by
a stream. The building work took a year, and he finally
moved in spring 761.

'Roots': The Japanese Occupation of Hong Kong started
on 25 December 1941 and lasted for three years and eight
months. The population of Hong Kong dwindled from
1.6 million in 1941 to 600,000 in 1945. Strict rationing
was imposed, causing many to die of starvation. My
grandparents survived but lost their metal shop and
everything they owned at gunpoint.

'Hero Tree': the quotation is from Ezra Pound's
translation of Confucius's *The Great Digest*.

'*China Landscape* in the Forecourt of the British Museum': *China Landscape* was an outdoor exhibition at the British Museum in 2008. The calligrapher Zhao Yizhou inscribed the Chinese character 華 on the scholar's rock.

'BN(O)': British National (Overseas) is a category of British Nationality created after the Sino-British Joint Declaration (1995) signed by Margaret Thatcher and Deng Xiaoping.

'Reading Thom Gunn's Notebooks at the Bancroft Library': the fourth stanza opens with a line from Book Six of Wordsworth's *The Prelude*, where the poet described his disappointment at finding that he had already crossed the Alps.

'Handwriting': the first stanza draws on Joyce's *Ulysses*.

'Watershed': the last line is the opening of *Hamlet*.

'Obstacles to Dreams': the quotation is from *The Tempest*.

'Ghost Letter': see 'The Letter of Lord Chandos' by Hugo von Hofmannsthal.

'Four Treasures of the Scholar's Studio': the four treasures are a brush, ink, ink stone, and paper.

ACKNOWLEDGEMENTS

I am grateful to the editors of *Acumen, Envoi, London Magazine, Magma, Poetry London, Poetry Review, Poetry Wales, The Rialto, The Warwick Review* and *The Wolf*, in which earlier versions of these poems were printed.

'Thatched House Destroyed by an Autumn Storm' won a *Times* Stephen Spender Prize for Translation in 2006 and was published in the prize booklet.

I would like to express my gratitude to the Arts Council UK and the British Library for recording some of these poems as part of their series, 'Between Two Worlds: Poetry and Translation'.

I would like to thank the School of English at the University of Hong Kong and the HKU Culture & Humanities Fund for sponsoring HKU Poetry Prize, and Hong Kong University Press and Impressions Design & Print Ltd. for producing the book.

I am indebted to Anna Armstrong, Matthew Betts, Mimi Ching, Mahlet Getachew, Saskia Hamilton, Hugh Haughton, Louise Ho, Ffiona Lewis, Jessica Murray, Adam Phillips, Jayan Prakash, Lorraine Ng, Christopher Reid, Page Richards, Fiona Sampson, and Brian Seibert who have accompanied and helped the traveller at different junctions.

ABOUT THE HKU POETRY PRIZE

The HKU Poetry Prize, initiated by the School of English at the University of Hong Kong in 2010, is an international award recognizing outstanding poetry written in English. Judged by renowned poets, it celebrates a body of original work in a first book of poems published by Hong Kong University Press. The HKU Poetry Prize looks to the history of poems and honours the craft and achievement of contemporary poets.